DRAWING DAVID DAICHES

Talbot Rice Gallery · The University of Edinburgh

24 April – 29 May 2004

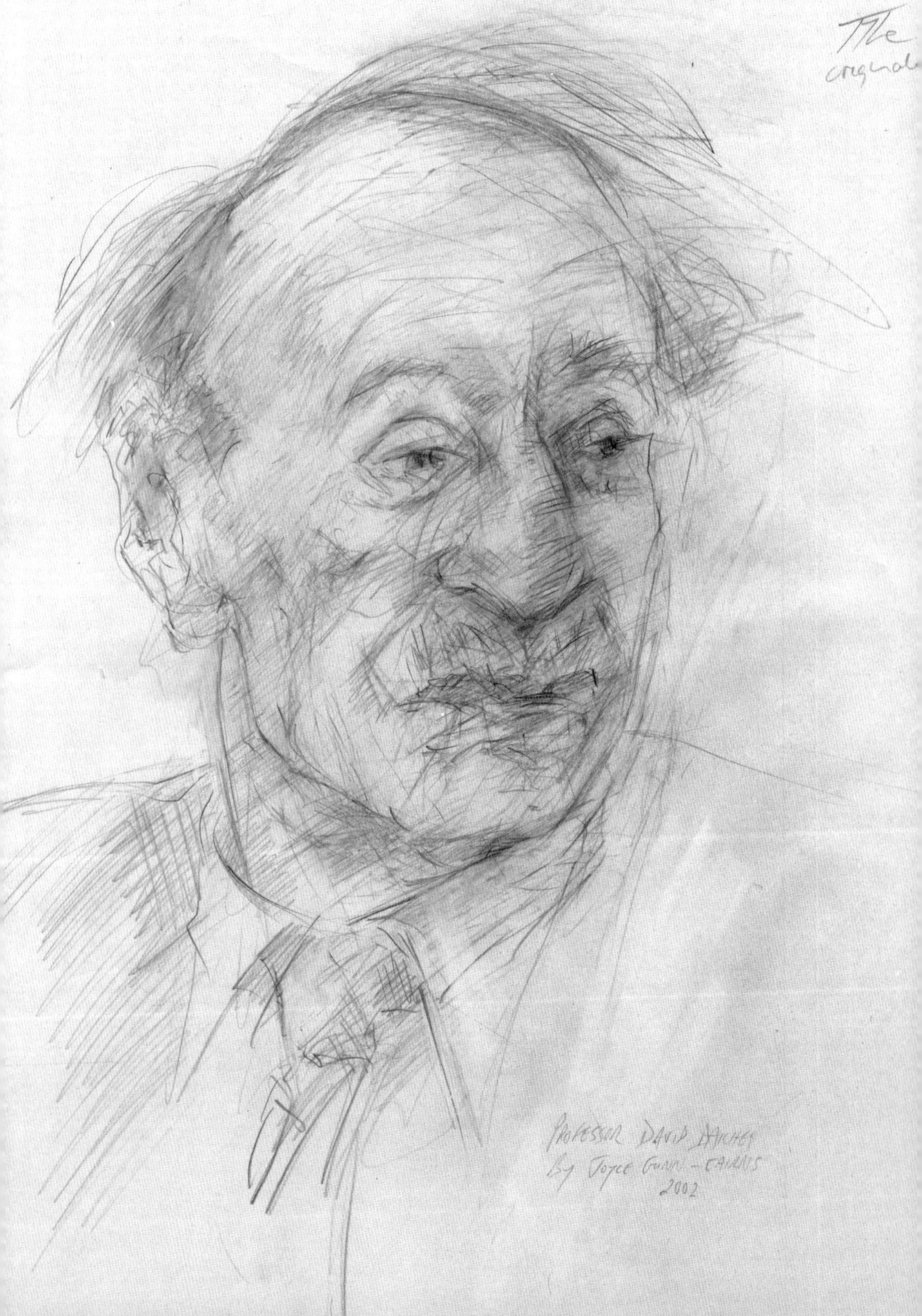
The
PROFESSOR DAVID DAICHES
By Joyce Gunn-Cairns
2002

PORTRAIT DRAWINGS BY

JOYCE GUNN-CAIRNS

DRAWING DAVID DAICHES

EXTRACTS FROM WRITINGS BY

DAVID DAICHES

TALBOT RICE GALLERY

EDINBURGH 2004

Published by Talbot Rice Gallery
for the exhibition *Drawing David Daiches*, 24 April to 29 May 2004

ISBN 1 873108 43 5

Printed in Scotland by Inglis Allen, Kirkcaldy
Designed and typeset in Adobe Caslon by Dalrymple
Endpapers by Jonathon Gibbs

Talbot Rice Gallery · The University of Edinburgh · Old College
South Bridge · Edinburgh EH8 9YL
Telephone 0131 650 2210 · E-mail info.talbotrice@ed.ac.uk
Fax 0131 650 2213 · Website www.trg.ed.ac.uk

Scottish
Arts Council

Thanks are warmly extended to all those who have helped make this celebration possible: The Hope Scott Trust, Edinburgh; Iain Black, Edinburgh; Jenni Calder, South Queensferry; Simon Coke, Edinburgh; Stewart Conn, Edinburgh Makar, Edinburgh; Eric Dickson, National Library of Scotland, Edinburgh; Prof. Douglas Dunn, University of St Andrews; The Eighteenth-Century Scottish Studies Society; The British Society for Eighteenth-Century Studies; The Mary Erskine School, Edinburgh; Prof. David Hewitt and Mrs Hewitt, University of Aberdeen; The Scottish Jewish Archives Centre, Glasgow; Julie Lawson, Scottish National Portrait Gallery, Edinburgh; Prof. Douglas Mack and Mrs Mack, University of Stirling; W. W. Norton & Co, New York and London; Dr James Reid-Baxter, Luxembourg; Jennie Renton, *The Scottish Book Collector*, Edinburgh; Prof. Alan Riach, University of Glasgow; Rt Hon. Sir Malcolm Rifkind, Inveresk; George Watson's College, Edinburgh; The Scottish Universities' International Summer School, Edinburgh.

· FOREWORD ·

'There are some philosophers who imagine we are every moment intimately conscious of what we call our SELF; that we feel its existence and its continuance in existence; and are certain, beyond the evidence of a demonstration, both of its perfect identity and simplicity.' So writes David Hume in the *Treatise of Human Nature*. He then goes on to examine this idea of the self and to conclude trenchantly that, far from being something of 'perfect identity and simplicity', where we seek the self there is actually 'nothing but a bundle or collection of different perceptions, which succeed each other with an inconceivable rapidity, and are in a perpetual flux and movement'. We look into ourselves and find, not certainty, but flux.

Thus Hume points to a paradox at the heart of western thought as it has evolved in northern Europe since the Reformation. So much in Protestantism and in the democratic tradition to which it gave rise is posited upon the idea of the individual, yet the individual is forever elusive. For several centuries, too, the importance of the individual made portraiture the art form closest to the heart of western ideas. But portraiture has at its heart the same problem; if Hume's paradox applies to the self, by how much more does it apply to our knowledge of others? Even appearances change moment by moment. Any likeness has to be a kind of generalisation, but how, logically, can you generalise about an individual? Inevitably as time has passed and the truth of what Hume said has grown more evident, portraiture has become more and more difficult. However, as Joyce Gunn Cairns demonstrates in her wonderful drawings of David Daiches, true and moving portraiture is still possible if the artist manages, as she has done, to find a way to take all this into account.

Hume himself counted the greatest portraitist of the age, Allan Ramsay, among his closest friends and Ramsay left us two memorable images of the philosopher. But if we look at Ramsay's account of his friend, especially the later of the two portraits, now in the Scottish National Portrait Gallery, we see how Ramsay was as conscious as the philosopher himself of this paradox at the heart of his own art. In the picture, Hume is half in shadow. He is elusive. On the point of dissolving back into the darkness, his image seems held together only momentarily by the power of the artist's imagination; and if in that portrait Ramsay pays tribute to his friend, in the way it is lit he also pays tribute to the artist who, even before Hume, had examined all this and come to the same conclusion as the philosopher. In his self-portraits Rembrandt returned again and again to examine himself and found there each time, not constancy, but elusive variety.

My own awareness of these complexities at the heart of the western experience and of the part played in them by Hume and the other great thinkers of the Scottish Enlightenment was stimulated by reading a small book that David Daiches published in 1964, *The Paradox of Scottish Culture.* It was a set of lectures, the Whidden Lectures, that he had delivered in Canada in that year. He had of course explored these ideas elsewhere and has done so since; but here, like one of the great texts of the Enlightenment, James Hutton's synopsis of his *Theory of the Earth*, the very brevity of the book is part of its imaginative power. An acorn is the synopsis of an oak tree and in the small compass of just a hundred pages, with extraordinary breadth of learning brilliantly condensed, Daiches described the great ramifying plurality of Scottish eighteenth-century culture; and, as he did so, he identified the paradoxes that he saw at its heart and that gave him his title.

The strength of this little book is the way the author roots his argument in his detailed knowledge of the particular circumstances of Scotland at the time; but as I reflected on it, it seemed to me it also opened up an argument with a much wider bearing on the problematic evolution of modern art and that the paradox of self identified by Hume was at the heart of it. Now, fittingly, Joyce Gunn Cairns's drawings are a tribute to David Daiches that seems to fit exactly in that frame.

Acutely aware of the problem of portraiture and of the elusiveness at its centre, her drawings are in series. Only a few of the dozens that she does are kept. Most are thrown away, but together the survivors reflect a process, like life itself, not a state. Her response to her sitter is extended in time by their sequence. As they sit together and she draws, he talks. Moods change, appearance changes even. Her choice of drawing as a medium also reflects the truth she is trying to capture.

It is in the nature of drawing that we are closest to the artist's thought processes as the hand extends and articulates the mind's inquiry. But her chosen style of drawing seems almost tentative. Searching as much as finding, implicitly it seems to accept that whatever is put down can only be provisional. She never adopts the sweeping line of elegant execution that imposes the sharp contour of definition. If she did, the image would fall victim to the paradox. Its truth would be destroyed; its validity lost. Instead she shows, as Ramsay did before her, that, with tact and care, even Hume's paradox of identity can be described. Her sympathetic response to the age of her sitter is part of this too. In her description of the marks of time and experience, she reflects on the deeper truth of Hume's observation and on the mutability of human life itself.

This foreword is also an opportunity to thank the artist on behalf of the University of Edinburgh for the gift of one of these drawings which is the occasion for this publication in honour of her sitter and for the exhibition that accompanies it. The portrait of one of its most distinguished alumni is an important and valuable addition to the University's great collection of portraits. I must also thank Michael Lister for selecting and editing the eloquent and appropriately personal collection of passages from David Daiches's writings included here. Finally I must thank the generosity all the admirers of Professor Daiches whose contributions great and small have made this publication possible.

DUNCAN MACMILLAN
Curator, Talbot Rice Gallery

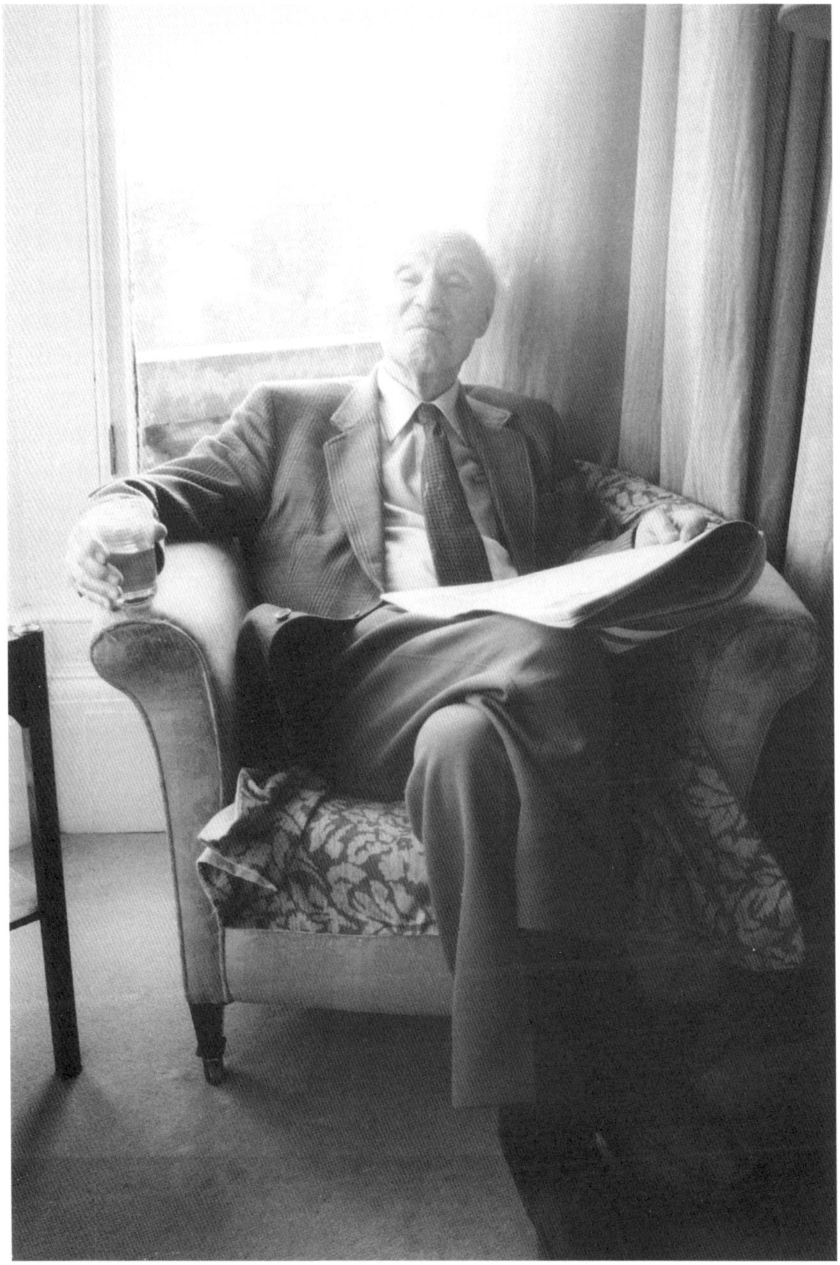

· PROFESSOR DAVID DAICHES ·

CBE FRSE FRSL DPhil Phd DLitt DUniv

David Daiches is one of Scotland's most distinguished writers. He is one of the major humanities scholars of the twentieth century. Regarded by Hugh MacDiarmid as the 'foremost living authority on our literature', David Daiches is 'probably the most senior literary critic and man of letters to enter the new millennium.'

Both a graduate and an honorary graduate of the University of Edinburgh, David Daiches first graduated from the university here seventy years ago. He is a Fellow of both The Royal Society of Edinburgh and The Royal Society of Literature. While David Daiches has spent the greater part of his professional life furth of Scotland – first in the USA and then in England – he is, without qualification, 'one of the great sons of Edinburgh, City and University.'

In multi-numerous areas within literary and cultural studies, David Daiches is an acknowledged expert, although, with characteristic humility, he nevertheless regards himself as a 'non-specialist.' He is an authority on Scottish, English, American and Anglo-Jewish literature and his work as a teacher has informed many, many generations of students on both sides of the Atlantic. As a more popular educator, Daiches has taken part in innumerable radio broadcasts, particularly on Radio 3, and before that the Third Programme, on Radio 4, and the earlier Home Service, and he has also appeared on television, in many arts and cultural programmes.

The contributions that David Daiches has made to literary studies, scholarship and to higher education are very significant indeed. In recognition of these contributions, Daiches was appointed a CBE in 1991 and more than a dozen universities and colleges across the world have conferred on him honorary professorships, doctorates and fellowships. These include: Edinburgh, Sussex, Stirling, Glasgow, Brown, Guelph, Sorbonne, Bologna, etc.

Born in 1912, Daiches came to in Edinburgh in 1919, when his father was appointed Rabbi of the Edinburgh Hebrew Congregation. Rabbi Dr Salis

Daiches held this post until 1945 and was 'virtual though not nominal' head of the Scottish Jewish community. Salis Daiches was born in Vilna in 1880 of a most distinguished line of rabbinical scholars. A talmudic scholar, whose Leipzig doctorate was on Kant and Hume, his lifelong ambition was to establish the Jewish community in Scotland as a full and recognised element in Scottish demography and Scottish culture. In 1991, a new housing development in Edinburgh was named after Rabbi Dr Daiches. This was the first street in Scotland to be called after a rabbi – probably the first street in Britain! His father's lifelong ambition had been, in part, achieved.

A graduate, *magna cum laude*, of Edinburgh University, David Daiches received his doctorate at Oxford, where he was Fellow of Balliol College, before going to the United States where he was Assistant Professor at Chicago, from 1937–43, and then Professor at Cornell, from 1946–51. He returned to Britain in 1951 to teach at Cambridge, where he was also a Fellow of Jesus College. During the war years, Daiches was Second Secretary at the British Embassy in Washington. Following Cambridge, he was one of the founding fathers of the University of Sussex, where he was Professor of English from 1961–77, and Dean of the School of English and American Studies there from 1961–68. From 1980–86 he was Director of the Institute for Advanced Studies in the University of Edinburgh.

As literary critic and cultural historian, in addition to his more than two hundred journal articles and research papers, Daiches has published over seventy scholarly works and critical studies. These include his earliest pioneering critical studies of modernist writers and poets; an important study of the development and sources of the King James Bible; critical studies of Virginia Woolf – Daiches was the first scholar ever to write a full critical discussion of Woolf's *Mrs Dalloway* in *The Novel and The Modern World*, and this was therefore the first consideration of the novel by a literary critic in book form; critical works on Milton and Boswell; pioneering revaluations of Burns, Scott and R. L. Stevenson, whose reputations Daiches brought out of the doldrums and whom he restored as writers of critical importance; essays, lectures and studies on a variety of aspects of Scottish literature and Scottish cultural history, including modern Scottish poetry, and particularly in the field of Scottish 18th century studies. In 1988, Daiches became the first recipient of The 18th Century Scottish Studies Society Lifetime Achievement Award for his outstanding contributions to the field, and the following year he received from The Saltire Society its prestigious Fletcher of Saltoun Award for distinguished services to Scotland. David Daiches has also written three works on Scotch whisky, the fruit of empirical and sober research.

Daiches's most personal writing is found in his *Two Worlds* and *A Third World*, both autobiographical works, and in his semi-autobiographical creation *Was*. *Two Worlds* is an essay in autobiography about the two childhood worlds that Daiches inhabited comfortably and cherished equally, his Jewish world and his Scottish world, and which illuminates his Edinburgh of the 1920s and '30s.

In honour of his contributions to Scottish literary and cultural studies, the Scottish National Portrait Gallery in 2001 acquired for its 'Eminent Scots' collection a portrait of Professor Daiches by Joyce Gunn-Cairns. Both Balliol College, Oxford and Jesus College, Cambridge, have portrait drawings of Daiches by Joyce Gunn-Cairns in their official College collections of portraits of distinguished Fellows.

In addition to this selection of portrait-drawings, this catalogue includes extracts from some of the writings of David Daiches. Both this exhibition and this catalogue are presented as a tribute to David Daiches, whose life's work has been devoted to the study and communication of literature, which stimulates us mentally and intellectually and instructs us morally and spiritually.

MICHAEL LISTER

THERE is no single 'right' method of handling literary problems, no single approach to works of art that will yield all the significant truths about them ... While the scrutinizing of literary theories is a valuable philosophical activity that can not only throw light on the nature of literature but also help us to read individual works with greater understanding and appreciation, the active appreciation of literature is not always dependent on such theorizing ... Art is greater than its interpreters ... All criticism is tentative, partial, oblique ... Art is meant to be experienced, and in the last analysis the function of criticism is to assist that experience ... To enjoy with discrimination, to discern value, to recognize and reject the spurious, to respond maturely to the genuine, never to be fooled by the shabby and the second-hand – that is the civilised approach to the arts. We turn to criticism to develop and strengthen that approach, ... criticism can come to this task directly or indirectly, through a frontal attack on individual literary works, through theoretical discussion of the nature of literary value, through investigation of origin and growth and causation. Every effective literary critic sees some facet of literary art and develops our awareness with respect to it; but the total vision, or something approximating it, comes only to those who learn how to blend the insights yielded by many critical approaches.

from CRITICAL APPROACHES TO LITERATURE, 1956

IT was in the beginning of 1919 that we moved to Edinburgh from Sunderland, where I was born, and that move was the true beginning of my life as I remember it; for I remember my childhood as a developing relation between family tradition and my sense of Edinburgh ... apart from a few fragmentary recollections of my Sunderland days, my remembered life begins in that timeless Spring of 1919, when I romped through the Edinburgh streets with all my senses wide open and with no preconceptions as to what I should find; and in the background my father, writing in his study, setting out to attend a meeting or conduct a service, and at the weekend gathering his family together to remind it of its identity and its heritage and to fortify its pride.

from TWO WORLDS, 1956

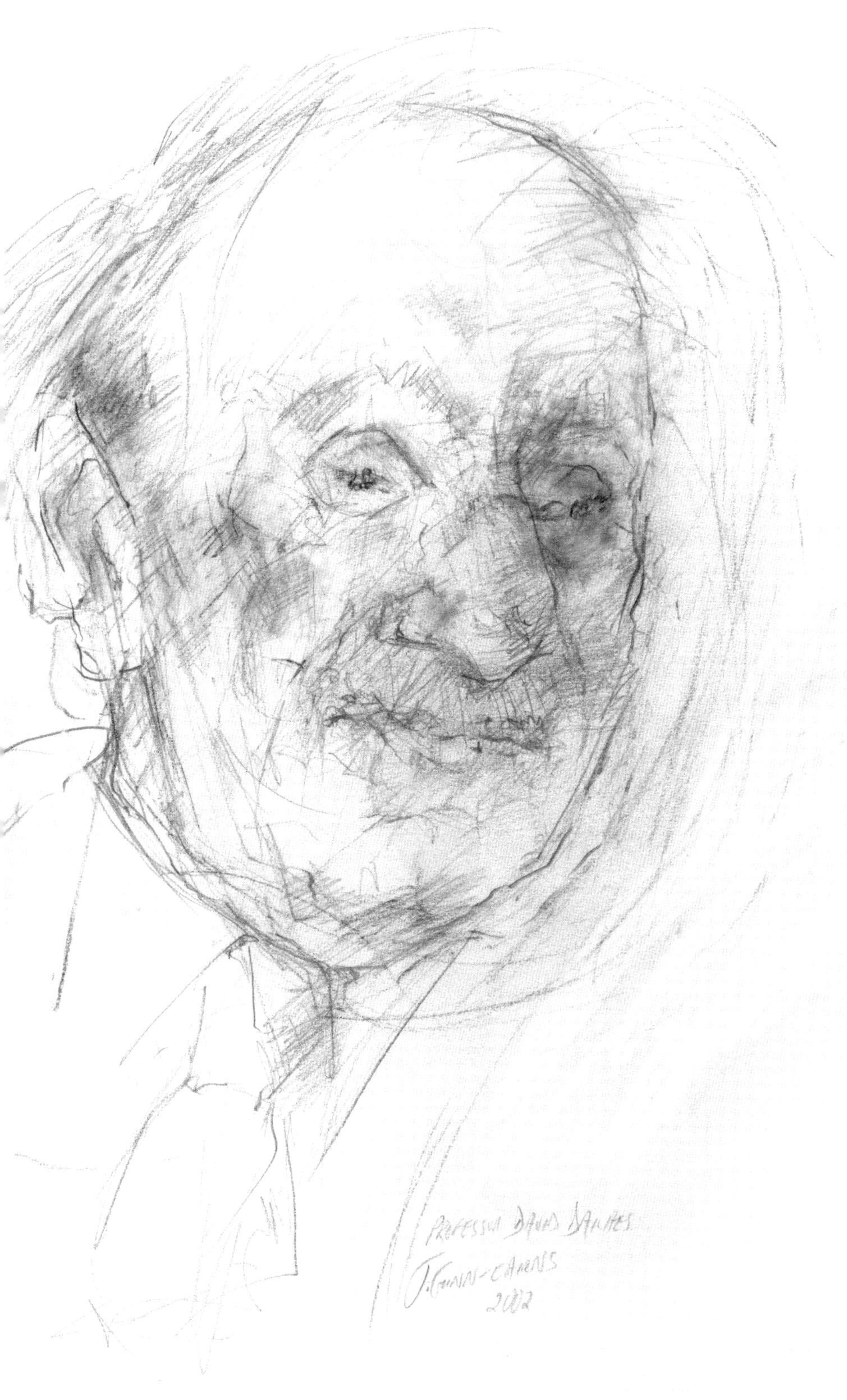
PROFESSOR DAVID DAICHES
2002

ONE day, without my knowledge, my father brought my notebook of poems to school and showed it to Dr Alison, [Headmaster of George Watson's College, Edinburgh], who referred him to Mr Findlay ... the head of the English department in the senior school. Mr Findlay liked some of the poems, and chose one ('To a fountain in moonlight', describing in a fairly complicated verse form a scene which I had never witnessed) to print in *The Watsonian*, the school magazine. *The Watsonian* was a dull, business-like magazine, with contributions by masters and senior boys; unlike some school magazines, it had no children's section in which to print crude and amusing effusions by youngsters. My poem, therefore, was not printed as an amusing or psychologically interesting example of a child's versifying: it was printed as a poem in its own right. I was both pleased and embarrassed. It was embarrassing to have my father talking about my poems and showing them to teachers and it was even embarrassing, in a way, to see something from my private notebook in print, to be read by my schoolfellows. But of course I was immensely proud – proud of my printed poem, and proud of my father's interest in my verses.

from TWO WORLDS

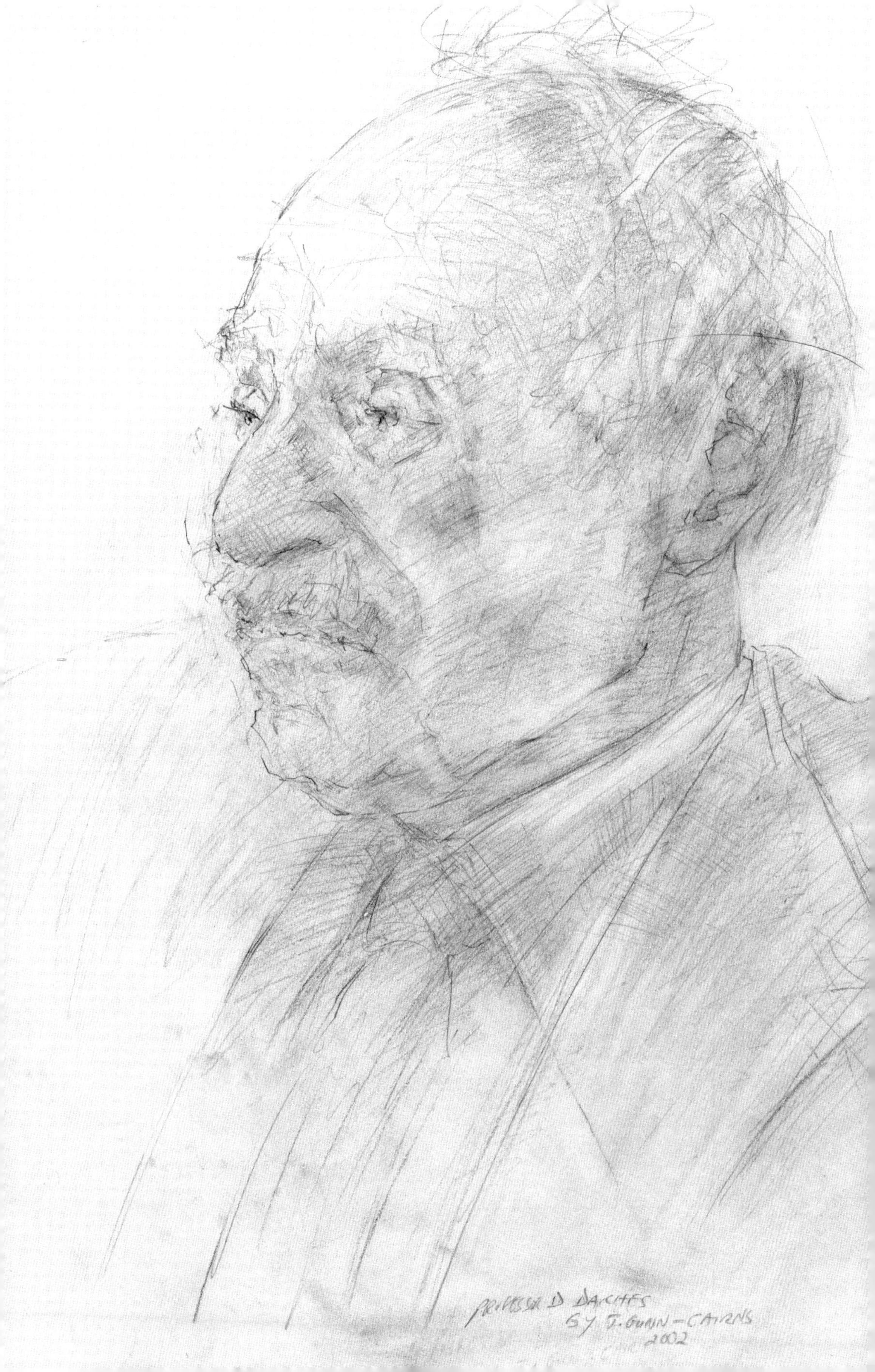
PROFESSOR D DAICHES
BY J. GUNN-CAIRNS
2002

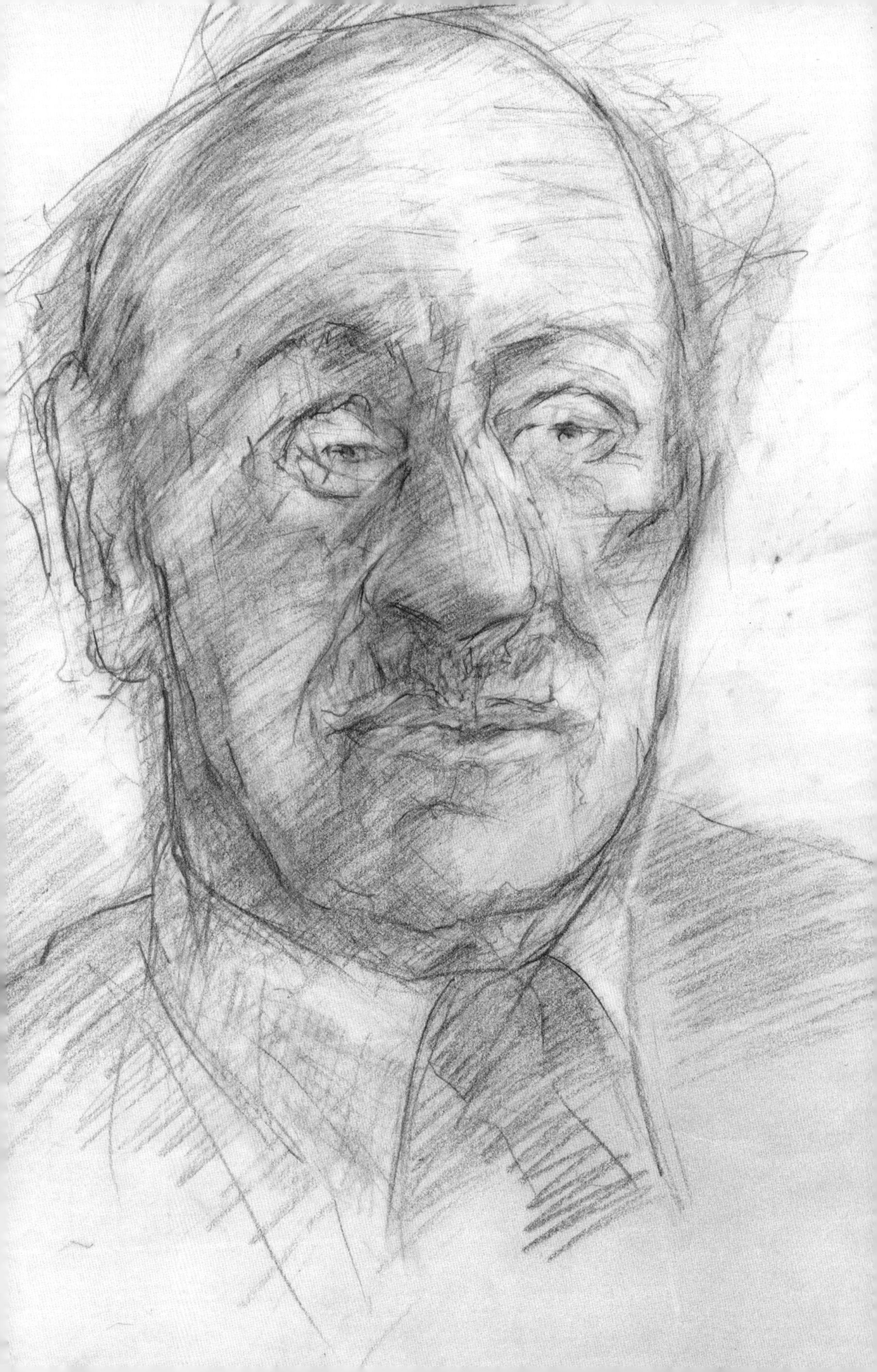

· *The Fountain in Moonlight* ·

Gleaming showers, gently spraying
Up into the air,
Glimmering softly in the moonlight,
With no other care
Than to be of other fountains
Fairest of the fair.

Sending upwards, higher ever,
Silvery drops of light,
Reaching nearly to the heavens
In the silent night:
With the dark blue sky above thee
What a lovely sight!

Shooting up thy rays of water,
Each a silver rod:
Dancing skyward, striving upward,
Singing praise to God:
Then thy drops below come falling,
Soaking through the sod.

D. Daiches (6 UJ), aetatis 11

from THE WATSONIAN, VOL XX, NO 1
DECEMBER 1923

You could also ask an innocent chum to say the word Puck while pulling the corners of his mouth apart with his fingers. This produced a dread word whose meaning nobody knew, but it was dread. Much dreader than simple mockery of institutions:

> Salvation Army free from sin / Went to heaven in a corned-beef tin.
> The tin was greasy, / They slipped out easy.

That, he knew, was not very witty and not very grammatical; but he enjoyed saying greasy with a long drawn-out vowel and a very zeddy s … In the Meadows these verses were ventilated in freedom and conscious daring. The young descendant of King David, or at least of generation upon generation of rabbis who had inhabited ancient Palestine, France, the Rhineland, Holland, Russia and God (literally) knew how many other countries before washing up in Scotland, trod those acres where once – let the historian tell what once. Where the Meadows now lie there lay for ages a loch coeval with that at Duddingston [ah, he knew Duddingston Loch well enough, and caught sticklebacks there, bringing them home in jars], some three-quarters of a mile from Lochrin, and where the old house of Drumdryan stands on the west, to the road that led to the convent of Sienna [that gave its name to Sciennes Road, his Sciennes Road, round the corner from his own street, and his father conducted Hebrew classes in the evening at Sciennes School – what would Our Lady of Sienna have said?] on the east, and about a quarter of a mile in breadth – a sheet of water wherein, in remote times, the Caledonian bull, the stag, and the elk that roamed in the great oak forests of Drumsheugh were wont to quench their thirst, and where, amid the deposit of marl at its bottom, their bones have been found from time to time during trenching and draining operations. The skull and horns of one gigantic stag (*Corvus elephas*), that must have found a grave amidst its waters, were dug up below the root of an ancient tree in one of the Meadow Parks in 1781 … The corvus elephas had drunk his fill where danced the moon in the great oak forest of Drumsheugh (great oak forest? genteel Drumsheugh Gardens in the West End of the New Town?). One stag that was never venison, whose flesh received no human benison, unsung by Scott, unrhymed by Tennyson.

from WAS, 1975

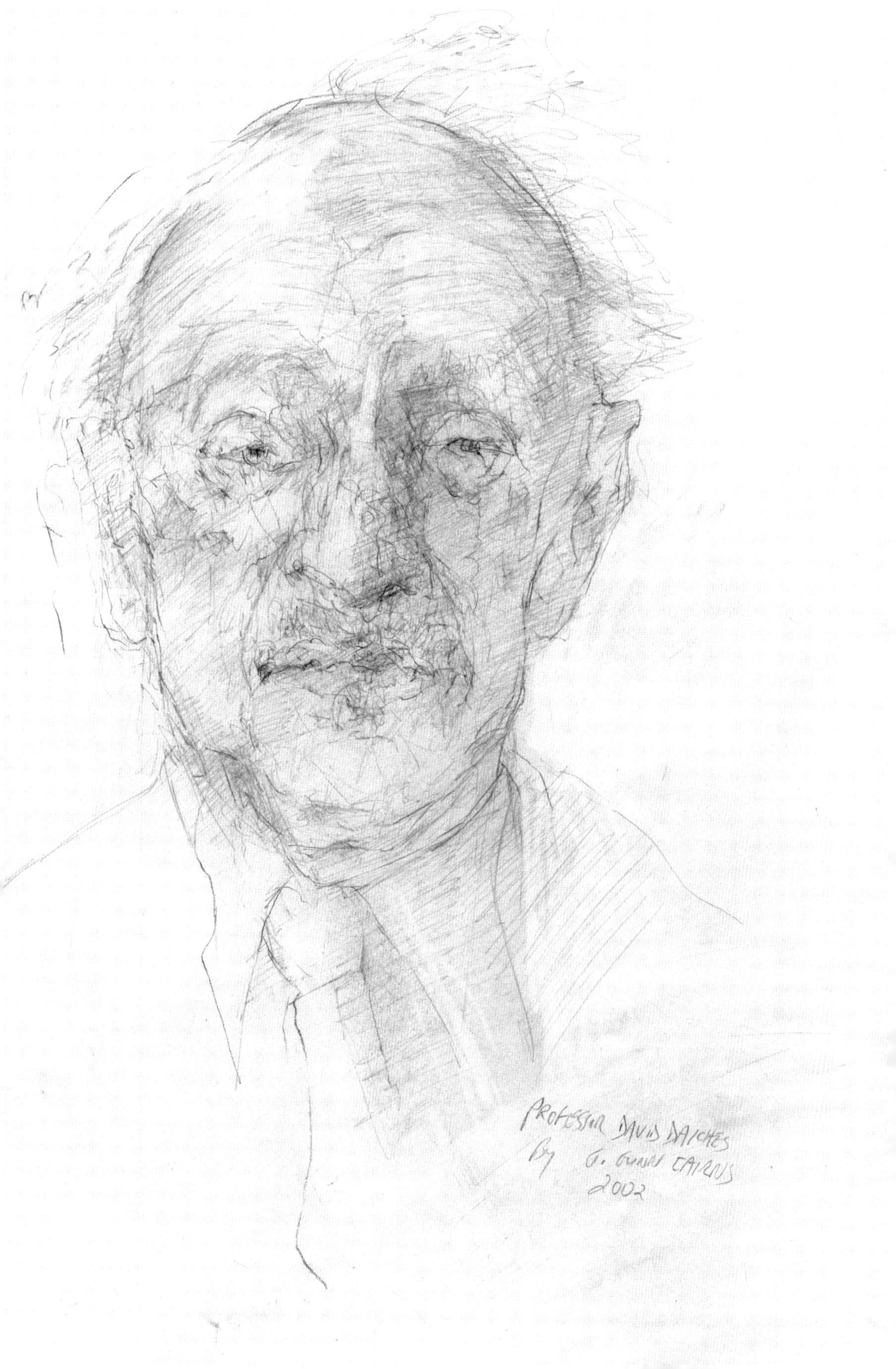
PROFESSOR DAVID DAICHES
By
CAIRNS
2002

... WORDS could create identities ... Yet, accustomed as he was from earliest childhood to hearing languages other than English spoken by visitors to the house, and having learned to read Hebrew perhaps before and certainly no later than he learned to read English, he knew that words had no unique and natural connection to their referents. At the same time shabbos was different from the sabbath, shul was a warmer and more familiar building than formal gentile-used synagogue, *frum* was certainly not the same as pious, and *yomtov* was something other than a festival ... Words could be sacred, and books and scrolls containing sacred words were also sacred. The scroll of the law read from each shabbos was sacred, and men kissed its exterior as it was carried round before and after the reading. It was a disturbing thing to drop a Bible or a prayer book, which had to be kissed on being picked up ... Here, in the realm of books, there really was a distinction between sacred and secular. But all books were good things; in his house reading in general was a good; and there was no expectation that he would read only sacred books on sabbaths and festivals. Those were the days, in fact, when, after the substantial midday meal consumed on the return from shul, he would ransack the bookcases in his father's study for a nineteenth-century novel or book on poetry with which he would settle down all afternoon, lost for hours in another world. Even school-books had their appeal, at least when they were examined for the first time. He would go to Thin's with the list of that year's required books ... How happy he was when no second-hand copy was available and he got a brand-new book, which was opened and examined on his return home with a special kind of excitement. Thin's itself was an enchanting shop, and he could spend hours just walking about there looking at books. Some boys got their books at Baxendine's, but his father had an account at Thin's, a bookshop which he considered far superior because of its greater size and greater variety of books displayed. Later he would browse among the open stalls of second-hand books at John Grant's in George IV Bridge, and pick up old copies of Nelson's classics for twopence or threepence a volume. He would pass Nelson's building on the way to Arthur's Seat, and the thought that that was where books were made was powerfully exhilarating. Books: he would cut up sheets of paper and sew them together, then invent a title to inscribe on the outside sheet and write anything that came into his head on the inside. He was making books. He would make in this way pocket diaries and dictionaries (one once got as far as the letter C) as well as collections of verses and even of advertisements … He wondered how books actually got printed and wondered if it would ever be possible for him to print his own books himself. He learned in school that the first printing press in Scotland was set up in Edinburgh by Walter Chepman and Andrew Myllar by licence of King James IV who fell at Flodden six years later … Our hero learned in school of Scott's involvement with Constable and with Ballantyne and of the eventual crash. Books could be dangerous, they could tempt to ruin. But that only confirmed his view that they were the most exciting things in the world.

from WAS

SOMEHOW 'The Cloud' found its way into a school reader he used in the term that began just after his seventh birthday, and for long he remembered the teacher reading and explaining the poem. He pored over it, and noted that it was said to be by P. B. Shelley. Peebee Shelley. In December 1919 the Chief Rabbi of the British Empire was visiting Edinburgh, and was entertained at his father's house. The Chief Rabbi, Dr J. H. Hertz, was proud of his familiarity with English literature and of his literary taste. In the course of a conversation over tea in the drawing-room he mentioned Shelley, and the little boy interrupted the grown-up conversation to ask: 'Do you mean Pee Bee Shelley?' The very reverend gentleman was much struck at this evidence of precocious familiarity with a great romantic poet, and the next week, as a Chanukah present, there arrived in the post for him a fat World's Classics edition of *Selected Poems of Shelley* bound in red leather. On the flyleaf the great man had written an inscription to him – to himself, by name – and signed it JHH. He realized you had to be very distinguished before you could sign your name with your initials only. He also felt he had won the book by false pretences. For 'The Cloud' was the only poem by Shelley he had ever heard of, and the only fact he knew about Shelley other than he had written this poem was that he was Pee Bee.

from WAS

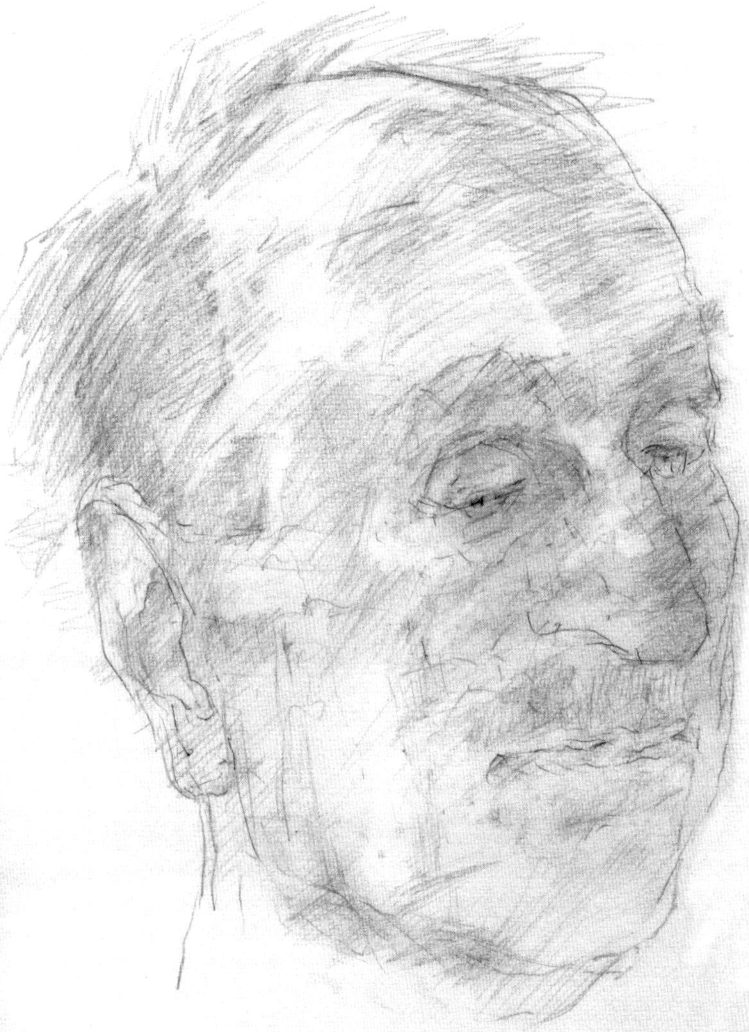
2002
DAVID DAICHES

Most of all he liked the concluding Friday evening hymn, *yigdal*, and the way in which the tune died away at the end of each verse: in winter especially, with the tiny congregation (not many came to the Friday evening service) singing in the four-fifths empty Graham Street synagogue he felt the singing of this hymn as an act of assertion, of identity, of continuity with the Jewish past; at the same time, walking out into the early dark of an Edinburgh winter, he thought it very much an Edinburgh winter song, and as he crossed the Meadows with his father and his brother with the strains of *yigdal* still ringing in his ears, the Hebrew hymn seemed to him bound up not only with Jewish history but also with Edinburgh Castle and the Vennel and that whole northern shore on which after so many centuries history had cast his family.

from WAS

This study of Burns is intended primarily as a critical examination of his poetic achievements rather than as a biographical work. However, in my endeavour to explain his development as a poet and the forces that helped to condition this development, I have been drawn to some degree into biography … I have tried to see Burns and his poetry in a wider context than that provided by traditional Burns studies. Interested as I am in contemporary developments in Scottish poetry and in the reassessment of Scottish literature that has been going on in Scotland for some time, I have perhaps given more attention to Burns' relation to the older Scottish 'makars' than most of his critics have done, and I have concerned myself, too, with the place of Burns in the Scottish literary tradition – a question much debated in Scotland these days. But my essential task has been to throw as much light as I can on Burns the poet, with a view to increasing understanding and appreciation of his poetry.

from PREFACE, ROBERT BURNS, 1950

In the sixteen years since this book was first published there has been a steady if hardly spectacular development of Burns scholarship and some interesting further attempts have been made to provide a revaluation of Burns' poetic achievements in the light of modern critical ideas and of the recent history and present needs of Scottish poetry ... But in spite of advances in scholarship and criticism, the same sentimental rubbish about Burns tends to be spouted forth each year by hundreds of Burns Night orators. The need for a critical study of Burns' poetry and for an estimate of the man and his work in the light both of objective critical standards and of the problems and pressures of his own time – and for that matter of the problems and pressures of *our* time – has thus not abated; if anything, it has grown. And that is one reason for the re-issue of this book.

from PREFACE TO THE 1966 EDITION

Since I wrote the Preface to the 1966 edition, James Kinsley's edition of the poems has appeared and established itself as the definitive text. Critical and scholarly work has continued to enrich our understanding of Burns both as man and poet ... The whole situation ... has developed in ways I hoped for but could not foresee when I originally wrote this book over thirty years ago.

from PREFACE TO THE 1981 REPRINT

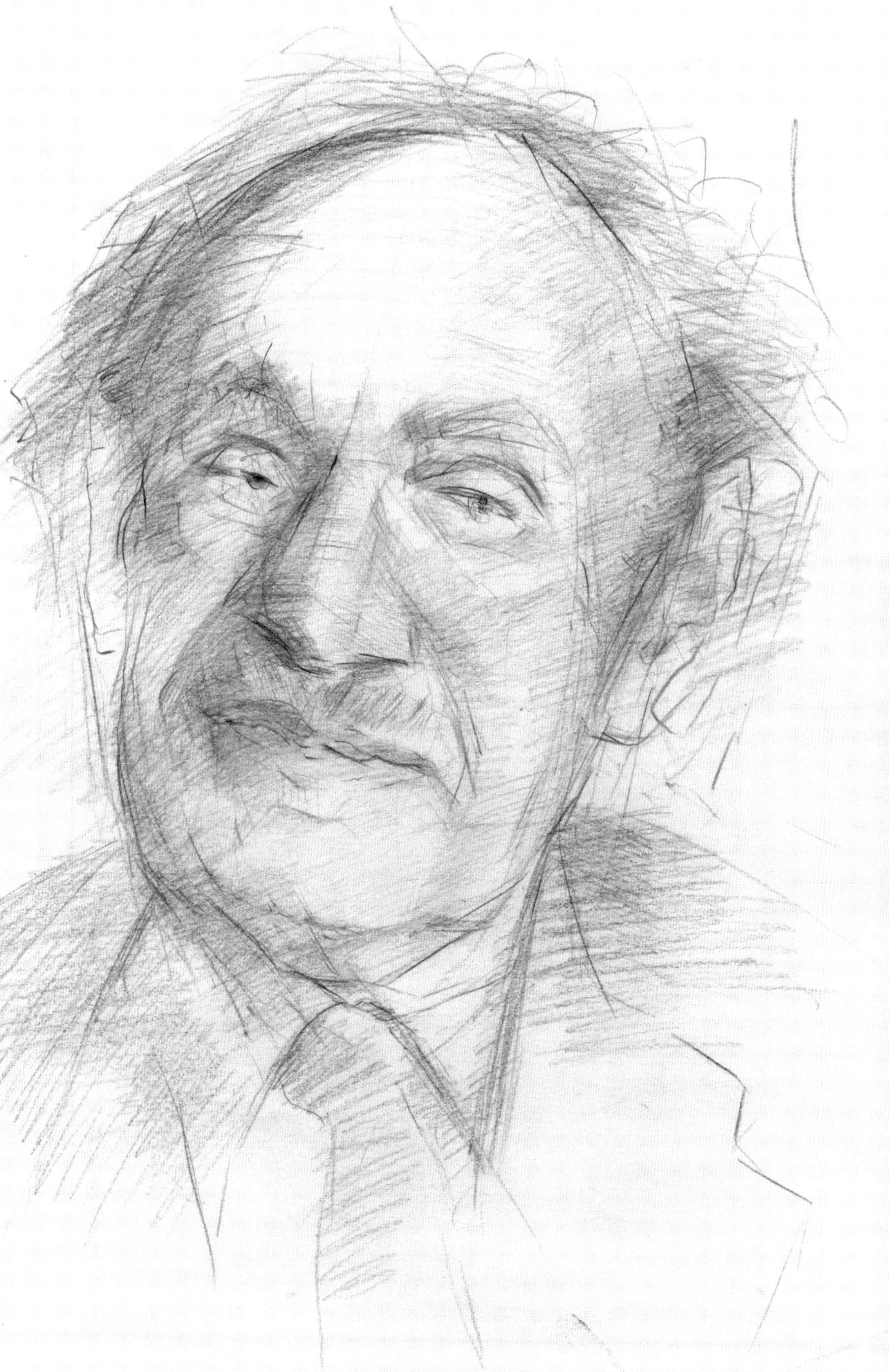

It is over a quarter of a century since this gallimaufry first appeared, breaking on a startled and incredulous Scotland with all the shock of a childbirth in church. Since then we have all grown more used to 'modern' poetry; when our author refers to Eliot's *Waste Land* we nod our appreciation, and the sudden transitions in mood and space which confront us so often are accepted on the analogy of Pound's *Cantos* or Auden's discursive pieces. Most of us no longer regard MacDiarmid and his poetry as still dangerous. The state of culture has caught up with him, we are inclined to think, and his methods are orthodox enough now.

But if we think this, we are dreadfully mistaken. In the first place, there is less in common between MacDiarmid and Eliot or Pound or Auden than there is between MacDiarmid and many an older classic. His technique is not 'modern' in the sense in which expositors of modern poetry now use the term; his obscurity is quite unlike the obscurity of *The Waste Land* or the *Cantos* (if indeed obscurity is the proper word at all); he has not Eliot's interest in the poetic potentialities of religious faith or Yeats' concern about symbols or Auden's gift for metaphysical clowning or Dylan Thomas's cunning cultivation of the elemental. His ancestors are not Hopkins and Laforgue and the Jacobean dramatists or any of the other well known sources of modern poetic idiom; but Chaucer and Dunbar and Villon and Skelton, the Goliardic tradition of the Middle Ages, the flyting tradition of mediaeval Scotland, the humanist polemics of Renaissance Europe. Indeed, there is more of Milton's Sonnets 'I did but prompt the age to quit their clogs' and 'On the New Forcers of Conscience under the Long Parliament' in much of MacDiarmid than there is of the French symbolists or the seventeenth-century metaphysical poets. MacDiarmid, in fact, remains wholly original in the sources of his poetic inspiration and in the special qualities of his poetry. He is still original, and he is still dangerous ... 1926 was a pretty shabby moment in Scotland's history, and it is astonishing to think that it was in that confused and apathetic year that this challenging poem-sequence on Scotland first appeared. It is a kind of dream allegory where the poet visits Hell and finds that every feature of its landscape reminds him of home. Grotesque, passionate, meditative, violent, plangent and reminiscent by turns, the poem moves with a fine assurance and a rich vitality. And, for all its severity about modern Scotland, this is not a hopeless poem; time and again the poet seeks refreshment in the recollection of physical sensation and the challenging beauties of the physical world, the glories of sensation, remain. The silence invoked at the end is not the silence of the inanimate world or of death, but the silence of the man who has lost speech in experience. A nice piece of irony on which to end a dangerous poem.

from preface to A DRUNK MAN LOOKS AT THE THISTLE, 2nd EDN, 1953

THAT we need a new perspective on the history of Scottish literature, a patterning of its material at once richer and subtler, is surely beyond dispute. The question to which I wish to address myself is this: How are we to look at Scottish literature in order to discover that pattern, and what sort of pattern will it turn out to be? Which is tantamount to asking: How should Scottish literary history now be written? … In spite of the many individual essays devoted to a revaluation of the Scottish literary tradition that have appeared during the last twenty years or so, I am not sure that we can say that we have the critical tradition … I do not think we have had in Scotland a really lively critical tradition since the rhetorical school of Hugh Blair and Lord Kames in the eighteenth century. Careful critical studies of individual authors are now the great necessity. Perhaps I may be allowed to say that my own studies of Robert Burns and Robert Louis Stevenson were intended as humble contributions to that kind of critical revaluation on which the new historian of Scottish literature must depend. I should like to see full-dress critical studies of all the major and many of the minor Scottish poets. We talk so much of Dunbar and his importance for the history of Scottish poetry. Where is the great new critical book on Dunbar, or on any of the Middle Scots poets? We are producing editions, yes, and biographies, but the full-dress book-length critical revaluations have still to come. And the significant new history of Scottish literature waits for them.

from THE WRITING OF SCOTTISH LITERARY HISTORY
delivered before the Edinburgh branch of The Saltire Society,
11 December 1954

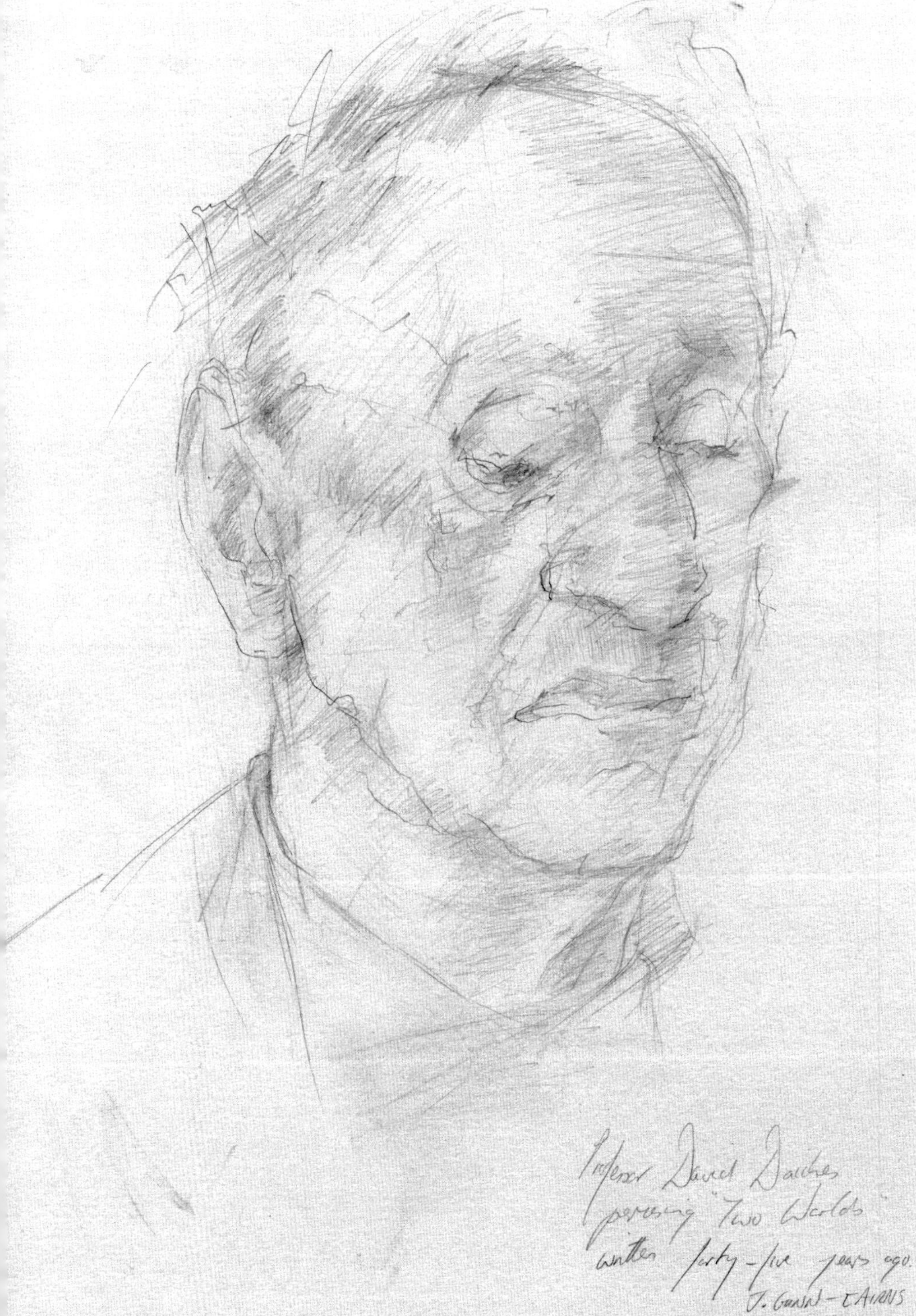
Professor David Daiches
perusing "Two Worlds"
written forty-five years ago.
J. GRANT-CAIRNS
2003

Scotch whisky is one of Scotland's great contributions to the good life. Like any alcoholic drink, it is capable of abuse, but the best guarantee against abuse is knowledge and discrimination. As we look back on its long story, remembering the farmer-distillers of the seventeenth and eighteenth centuries, the proud smugglers of the days when the Government was desperately fumbling for ways of taxing and controlling whisky production, the invention of the Coffey still and its momentous consequences, the flamboyant entrepreneurs of the later part of the nineteenth century, and the world-wide reputation of Scotch whisky today, we cannot but marvel at the way in which a spontaneous Highland activity which fitted in so well with the rhythms of the agricultural year has become over the years a vast industry. And I have my more personal memories: celebrating a wedding anniversary with fresh-caught salmon and a bottle of Glen Grant in the kitchen of a little house by the Moray Firth; landing up in a little Banffshire pub after a wet day's trout-fishing to warm myself with the spirit distilled all around me; talking with fellow writers and poets on a summer evening in a Rose Street pub in Edinburgh with drams of a variety of Highland malts standing on the bar between us; sipping Clynelish after dinner at home with a few academic friends as we planned the development of the University of Sussex; arriving at the house of a friend in New Jersey to find that he had ordered in some Mortlach because he knew I was coming and had heard that I liked that particular whisky; celebrating Hogmanay sitting on a bed in a hotel room in Agra with two friends and a bottle of Glenlivet after visiting the Taj Mahal by moonlight; drinking a nameless but obviously authentic blended Scotch from a lemonade bottle full of the liquor supplied by a friendly clerk at Belgrade airport as I waited a weary time for the airport to be cleared of the top brass and security officers awaiting the arrival of President Tito; drinking with courteous distillery managers at distilleries all over Scotland; and innumerable occasions, domestic, convivial, celebratory or merely casual, gratifying the palate and warming the spirit with this great drink. The proper drinking of Scotch whisky is more than indulgence; it is a toast to civilization, a tribute to the continuity of culture, a manifesto of man's determination to use the resources of nature to refresh mind and body and enjoy to the full the senses with which he has been endowed.

Let husky wheat the haughs adorn
An' aits set up their awnie horn,
An' pease and beans, at e'en or morn,
  Perfume the plain:
Leeze me on thee, John Barleycorn,
    Thou king o' grain!

To which we may add:

Freedom an' whisky gang thegither,
    Tak aff your dram!

from SCOTCH WHISKY, ITS PAST AND PRESENT, 1969

THE Scottish Enlightenment is a relatively recent term for the extraordinary outburst of intellectual activity that took place in Scotland in the eighteenth century. Some historians apply the term to the whole course of Scottish culture between the Union of 1707, when Scotland lost its separate political identity by joining with England in a common British state, and the death of Sir Walter Scott in 1832. This century and a quarter, however, covers too much change and diversity to be usefully considered as defining a single cultural movement. The latter half of the eighteenth century, perhaps a period as limited as 1760 to 1790, is more easily defensible as the true Golden Age. It was right in the middle of that period that the printer, antiquary and biographer William Smellie recorded an observation made by 'Mr Amyat, King's Chemist, a most sensible and agreeable English gentleman' who spent a couple of years in Edinburgh: 'Here I stand at what is called the *Cross of Edinburgh*, and can, in a few minutes, take fifty men of learning and genius by the hand.' Fifty men of genius, and that only in Edinburgh! Other Scottish cities, especially Glasgow and Aberdeen, produced their own geniuses, and the Scottish Enlightenment can be said to have begun in Glasgow with the publication of Francis Hutcheson's *Inquiry into the Originals of our Ideas of Beauty and Virtue* as early as 1724. But the movement in its heyday was centred in Edinburgh.

from THE SCOTTISH ENLIGHTENMENT – AN INTRODUCTION, 1986

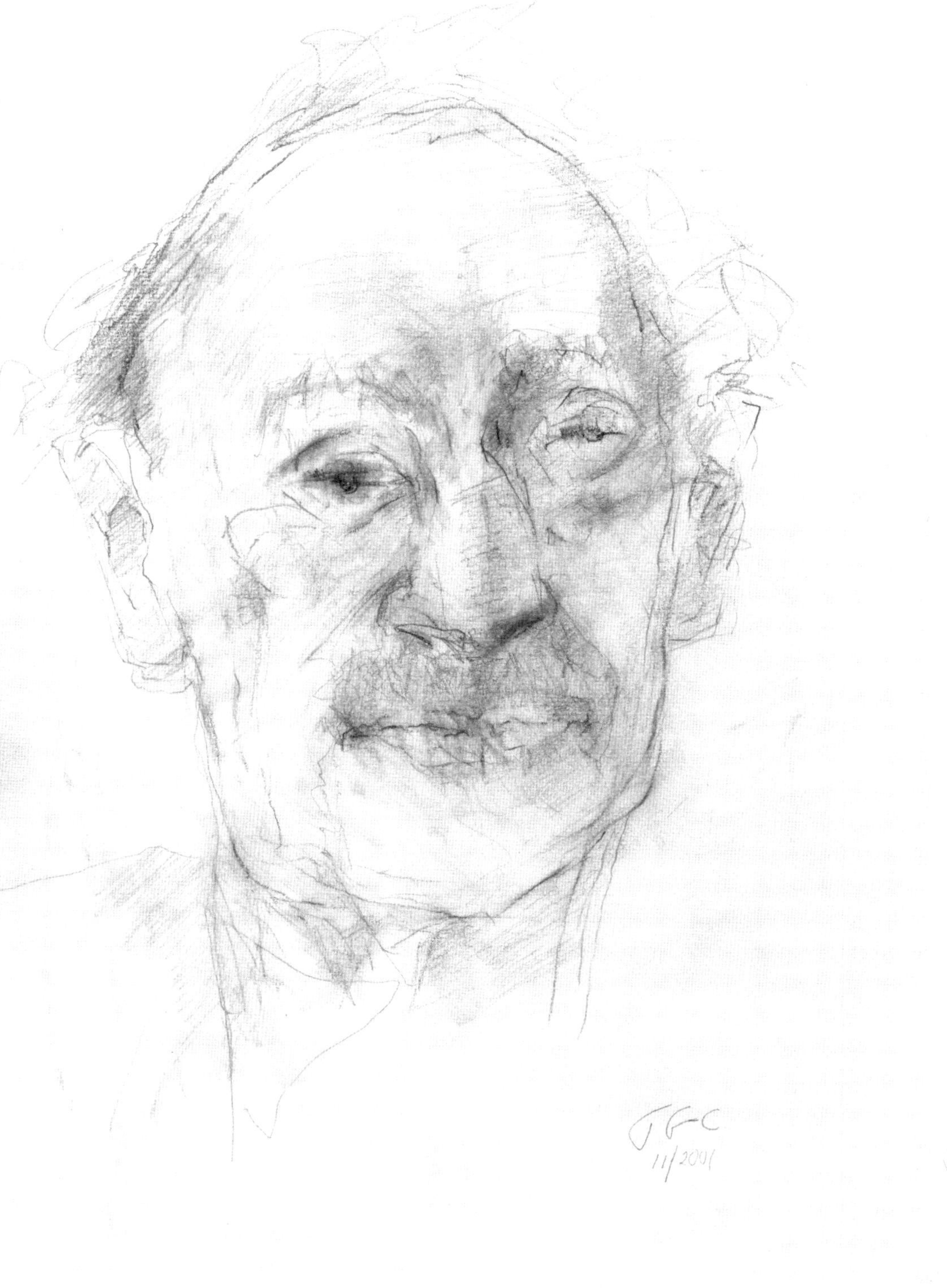
11/2001

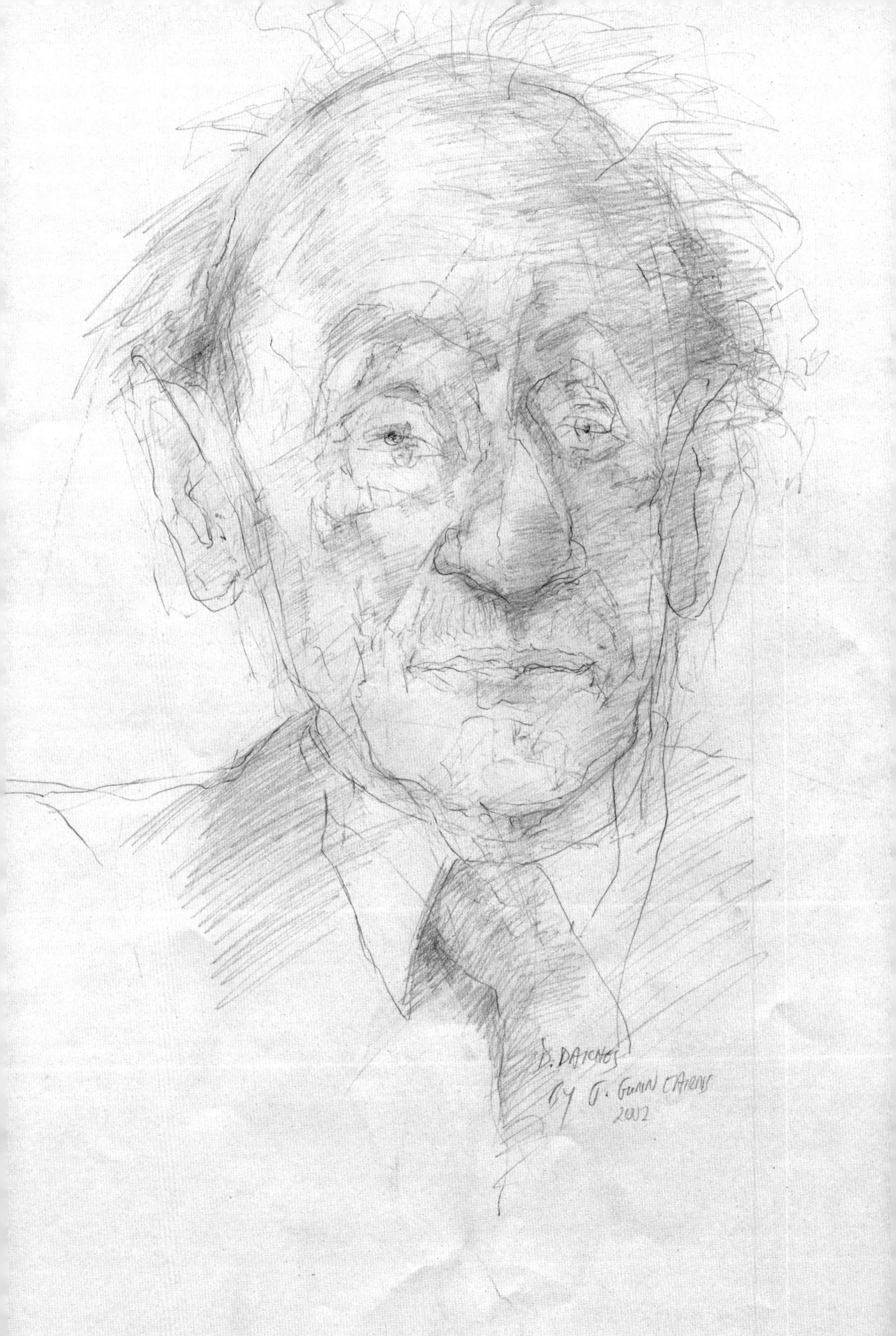
D. DAICHES
by G. Gunn Cairns
2002

It is one of the paradoxes of eighteenth-century Scottish thought that humane, enlightened and progressive thinkers tended to be politically conservative while the opposing Calvinists, with their hell-fire sermons and stern belief in election and predestination, were socially much more radical. If the emergence of Moderatism helped to produce an intellectual climate in which the Scottish Enlightenment could flourish, it also, by its emphasis on order and social hierarchy ... brought about its own decline. For Moderatism had nothing to offer in an age threatened by the French Revolution but what Lord Cockburn was to call 'a passive devotion to the gentry'. The great age of the Scottish Enlightenment could not cope with the new social and political ideas that emerged at the end of the century. Its optimistic belief in human benevolence and in the calm progress of an ordered society seemed to many to be irrelevant after 1789 ... Whatever happened to Moderatism by the end of the eighteenth century, there can be no doubt that its earlier emergence helped to make the Scottish Enlightenment possible or that many of the Moderates were themselves active in the movement. That Scottish intellectual culture would move in this direction after the achievements of the late seventeenth century in medicine, mathematics, and law, aided by the rise of Moderatism in religion, may seem a natural expectation to us looking back now, but in fact there were other directions in which at one time it seemed it might go. One was in the direction of a native Scottish humanism, a direction indicated by the life and work of Thomas Ruddiman ... In reaction to the union of 1707, the kind of nationalism represented by Ruddiman looked to the international language of Latin as Scotland's means of making its culture known throughout Europe and to the Scots language as a means of asserting Scotland's identity. Ruddiman worked with the printer and bookseller Robert Freebairn and with another patriotic Edinburgh printer James Watson in his career as editor and publisher of books calculated to restore Scotland's pride in her native traditions. He was also a Latin scholar ... whose edition (published by Freebairn) of Gavin Douglas's translation of the *Aeneid* ... is a remarkable piece of editing, with a glossary of Scots words that laid the foundation for Scots lexicography. Ruddiman also edited the *Opera Omnia* of the great sixteenth-century Scots humanist poet and scholar George Buchanan ... Ruddiman preceded David Hume as Keeper of the

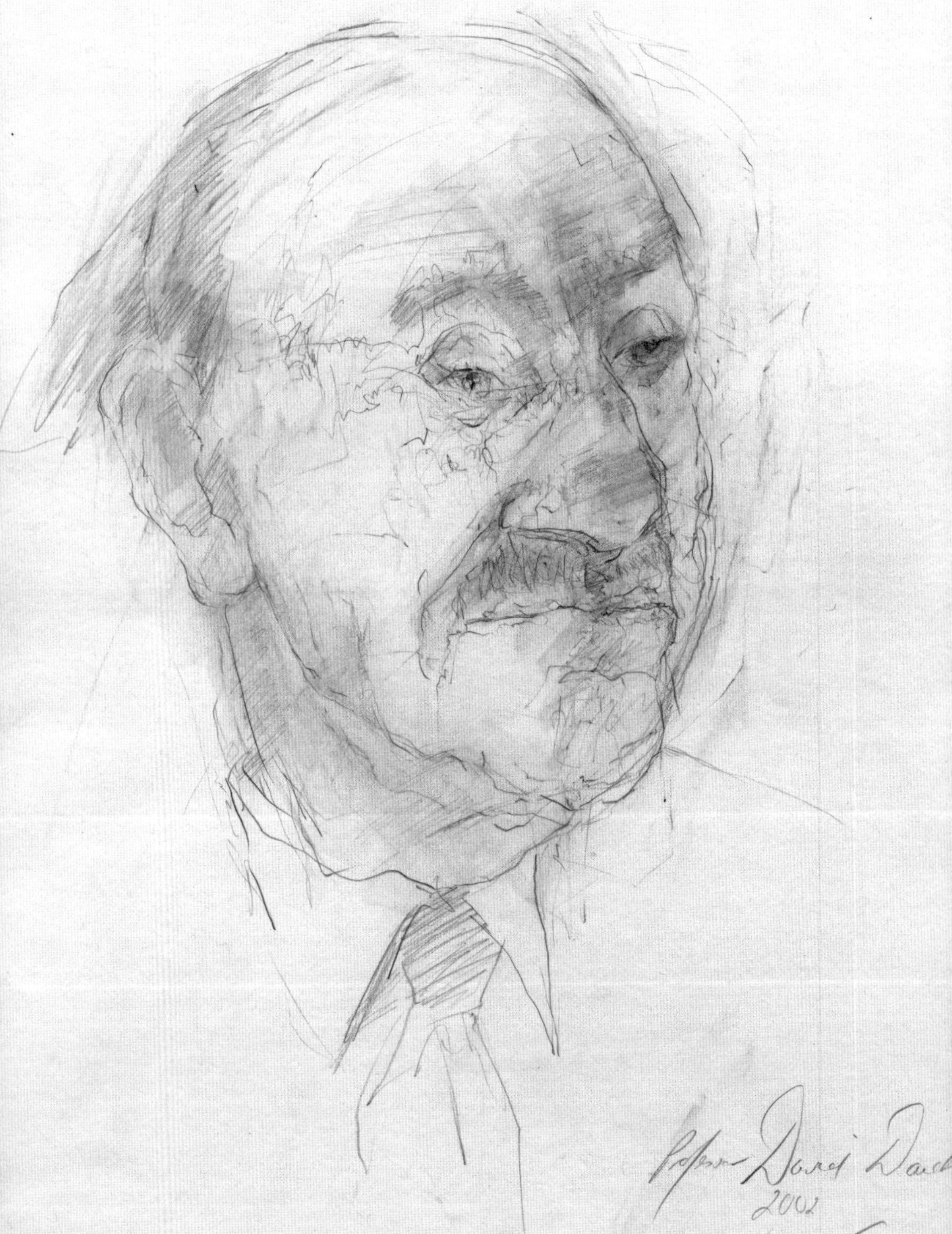
2002

Advocates' Library. He inspired a movement of Scottish patriotic publishing which at one time looked as though it would represent a major reaction to the Union. Ruddiman's vernacular humanism, as it may be called, was however not really a serious option for Scotland: it was altogether too late in the day for a Scoto-Latin culture. But its influence can be seen, however, indirectly, in the Scots poetry of Robert Fergusson and perhaps in the vernacular classical architecture of some Edinburgh building of the 1760s (George Square, for example) as compared with the more international classical style of Edinburgh's New Town, so much ... a symbol of the ideals of the Scottish Enlightenment.

from THE SCOTTISH ENLIGHTENMENT – AN INTRODUCTION

My last example comes from even further back. It is a poem – and it *is* a poem, though not generally thought of as one – which represents the old Hebrew priestly blessing. It invokes God with total authority and confidence. Its incantatory rhythms create a sense of communicating assurance of well-being and peace. It is, in a way, what we all want – a totally certain invocation, by someone whose communally agreed role it is to utter it, of divine good for us. When my father addressed a boy celebrating his bar mitzvah in the synagogue he always ended with these resonant Hebrew words of blessing:

May the Lord bless you and keep you.
May the Lord make his face to shine upon you and be gracious unto you.
May the Lord turn his face to you and grant you peace.

The power and beauty of these benedictory words transcend any question of belief in a personal God. The cadence of the repetitions, the incantatory effect, the sense of transmitting a force of good through an intermediary, the simple finality of that resting of that last word shalom, peace – this is poetry, *spoken* poetry, that goes behind and beyond questions of belief to express the universal yearning for reassurance and for some kind of personal relationship with the giver of that reassurance. Matthew Arnold said that more and more people would turn to poetry 'to interpret life for us, to console us, to sustain us', I doubt if his prophecy has been fulfilled to the degree that he anticipated. But poetry *can* have these functions, and this ancient priestly blessing can still console and sustain even those who do not share the faith of those who first framed it. The poetry of Old Western Man – and for that matter of Old Middle-Eastern Man – can still speak to us across the ages.

from GOD AND THE POETS. THE GIFFORD LECTURES, 1983

Pathetic Fallacy

Mist on the Downs. The garden end obscured.
The trees stand faintly out against the white.
A muted scene, at rest, complete, assured,
Matter of lines, relationships and light.

There is no meaning in the stance of trees.
Here is a truth we must undo: we must
Implicate nature in our reveries;
We need a neutral world to bear our trust;
We press our burdens on indifferent things.
Take that, and that! How unsolicited
Our gifts, what help the giving brings
To giver: out of need is fancy bred,
Till even the wind acquires a human call.

Our one imperative: as we slowly fall
Down to the final dissolution, know
We touch the earth with meaning as we go.

from EARLY POEMS *c.*1944 *in* A WEEKLY SCOTSMAN, 1994

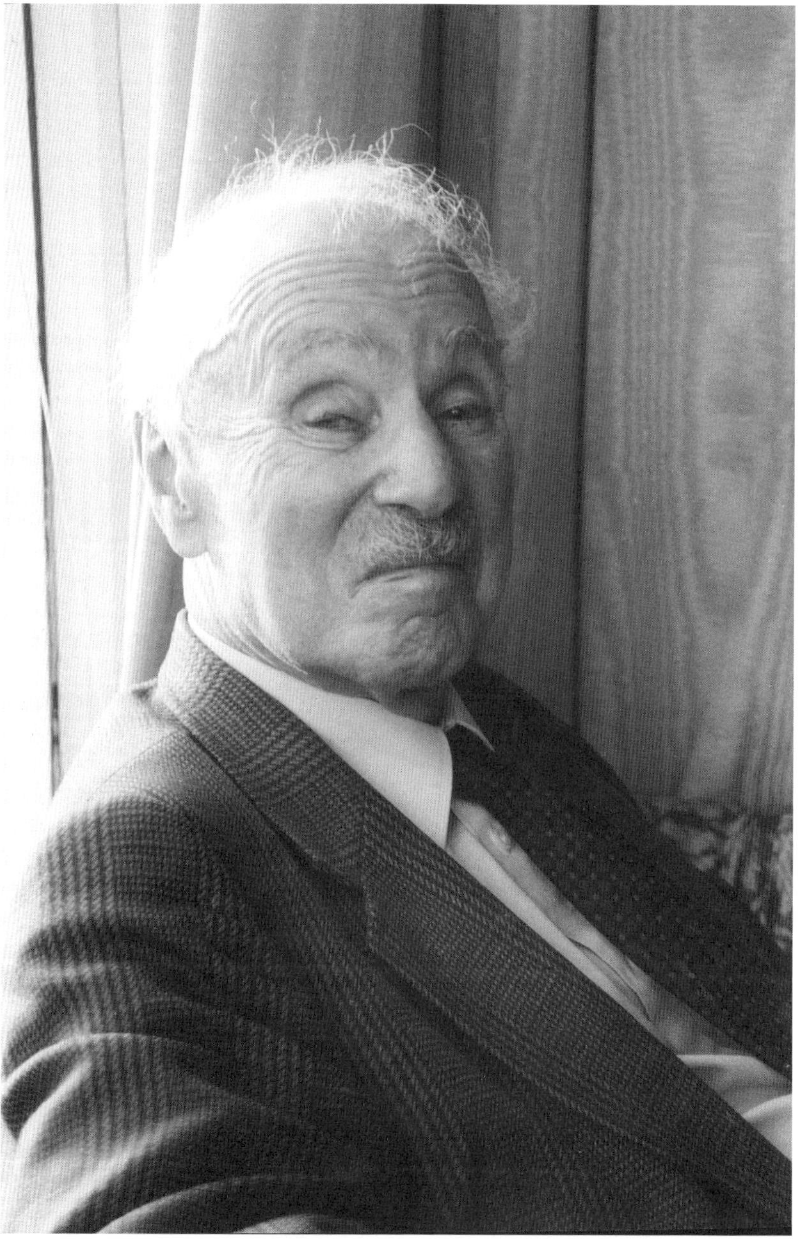

BIOGRAPHY & SELECT BIBLIOGRAPHY

William Baker's excellent 'David Daiches: A Bibliography, 1934–1978 ', in *Bulletin of Bibliography,* vol.36, no.1, accounts naturally for only the first 44 years of Daiches's publications; works post-1978 are still to be collated and listed. Both David Daiches's volumes of autobiography – *Two Worlds* and *A Third World* – as well as his semi-autobiographical creation *Was*, are, of course, essential reading.

1912 David Daiches born in Sunderland, 2 September

1919 Moves with family to Edinburgh, where his father had been appointed Rabbi of the Edinburgh Hebrew Congregation

First attends George Watson's College

1923 First poem, 'To a Fountain in Moonlight' published in *The Watsonian*

1930 Matriculates at University of Edinburgh

1932 Wins Vans Dunlop Scholarship and the Elliott Prize

1934 Graduates MA with Honours in English Literature

Assistant to Professor Dover Wilson

Publishes research articles on Donne and MacDiarmid

1935 Elected first Bradley Fellow, Balliol College, Oxford

Publishes his first book, *The Place of Meaning in Poetry*. The *Times Literary Supplement* praises the work, the reviewer recognizing that the subject matter of the work is 'important and difficult enough to justify repeated discussion.' Reviewed in the same issue of The *TLS* are MacDiarmid's '*Second Hymn to Lenin*' and William Soutar's *Poems in Scots*

1936 Publishes *New Literary Values: Studies in Modern Literature*. This book receives warm reviews from William Empson and Neville Coghill. In this book, Daiches speaks of 'the critic's duty to define the right relationship between literature and culture'

1937 Marries Isobel Janet Mackay, a former fellow-student from Edinburgh in Oxford

Awarded DPhil from Oxford for his thesis on the development and sources of the King James version of the English Bible of 1611 with special reference to the Hebrew tradition

David and Isobel Daiches leave UK for USA, for David to take up a teaching post at Chicago

1938 Publishes *Literature and Society*. Here, Daiches discusses the place of literature in human activity and the extent to which the nature and function of literature are determined by the social conditions under which the writer lives. Acknowledging that literature has a function and a value of its own in society, Daiches also sets out his belief of the critic's 'duty': 'to prevent the mass of the population from reading only trash and to stimulate the production of first-rate literature, and to ensure that everybody has the opportunity and the training to be able to share in our cultural heritage.' Written for Gollancz's Left Book Club, this work gives Daiches a left-wing reputation among his American students. C. E. M. Joad reviews this book in the *New Statesman*

1939 *The Novel and the Modern World*. This book is both praised and damned by the American critic Allen Tate, who holds it up as equally brilliant and dangerous. The chapter on Woolf's *Mrs Dalloway* is the first consideration (and full critical discussion) of that novel by any literary critic in book form

1940 Publishes *Poetry and the Modern World: a study of poetry between 1900 and 1939*. The *TLS* reviews this work very favourably, describing Daiches as 'a learned and courageous American critic.' The following month, The *TLS* prints a letter correcting the reviewer's misapprehension that the author is of American origin

1941 Publishes *The King James Bible: a study of its sources and development*. This work is based on Daiches's Oxford DPhil thesis

1942 Publishes *Virginia Woolf* – this study of Woolf is to be for many years the best introduction to her work

Wins the Quantrell Award ($1,000) for excellence in under-graduate teaching

1943–46 War service at British Information Service, New York, and subsequently as Second Secretary at the British Embassy, Washington

1946–51 Professor of English, Cornell University; becomes a member of the 'Vicious Circle', a select discussion-group

1947 Publishes *Robert Louis Stevenson – a revaluation*. This pioneering work gives Stevenson his proper due as a writer and acknowledges his great achievements

Co-founds, in Edinburgh, The Scottish Universities' International Summer School

1949–57 Regular contributor of poems and short stories to *The New Yorker*

1950 Publishes *Robert Burns*. A further pioneering work that concentrates on the development of Burns as a poet and thus represents a break from the more traditional treatment of the man. Reviewing it in *The Morning Star*, MacDiarmid welcomes 'this splendid volume [which] takes its place at the head of all literature on the subject'

Appointed University Lecturer at Cambridge, England and elected Fellow of Jesus College

1951 Daiches publishes his essay, ' Scott's Achievement as a Novelist'. This seminal essay 'rescues Scott from the cellar in which literary critics had imprisoned him' and 'sets the scene for the revaluation of Scott in terms which modern criticism has taken up'

Publishes *Willa Cather: A Critical Introduction*

Returns to UK to take up lectureship at Cambridge

1952 Appointed Honorary Member of The Irvine Burns Club (HRH Prince Philip also appointed in same year!)

1953 Writes introduction to second edition of '*A Drunk Man Looks at the Thistle*'

1956 *Two Worlds: An Edinburgh Jewish Childhood*, first published in the USA, and written partly in Chicago in 'a mood of pure self-indulgence', this work is to establish itself as a piece of socio-cultural Scottish history

Publishes *Critical Approaches to Literature*

Publishes *Literary Essays*

1957 Publishes *Milton*

1957–62 Fellow of Jesus College, Cambridge

1958 Elected Fellow of The Royal Society of Literature

1960 Publishes *A Critical History of English Literature*. A scholarly and analytical history of English literature in four volumes

1961 Co-founds The University of Sussex

1961–77 Appointed inaugural Professor of English and American Studies and subsequently Dean of the School of English and American Studies, University of Sussex

1961–85 Assumes general editorship of the *Studies in English Literature* series. Daiches's 'General Preface' to the first publication provokes *The TLS* to devote a leading article to the dangers of 'Close Study' and the creeping influence of the American 'New Critics.' *The TLS* , though with the profoundest of qualifications, does welcome the series

1962 MacDiarmid describes Daiches as 'the foremost living authority on our literature'

The Norton Anthology of English Literature first published. David Daiches is editor of the twentieth century section. This magisterial anthology is based on a literature course that both David Daiches and M. H. Abrams, its chief editor, devised and taught at Cornell University. Now in its 7th edition, *The Norton Anthology* remains perhaps the most comprehensive anthology of its kind and is unsurpassed as a text for under-graduate courses in English literature

David Daiches presides at the historic session on 'Scottish Writing Today' at the International Writers' Conference in Edinburgh. Daiches predicts 'interruptions for fights, abuse, differences of opinion and so on.' His predictions are correct when MacDiarmid and Trocchi, among others, cross claymores

1964 Publishes *The Idea of a New University: An Experiment in Sussex*. This is a blueprint for the creation of the new university

Publishes *The Paradox of Scottish Culture: the eighteenth-century experience*. Given first as the Whidden Lectures, McMaster University, Canada, this 'acute and stimulating book' according to G. E. Davie, 'opens up a rich territory for further study.' Norman MacCaig praises the writer's 'extremely discerning eye and the immense scholarship'

1968 Publishes *More Literary Essays*

1969 Publishes *Scotch Whisky, its past and present*

Publishes *Some Late Victorian Attitudes*. These three essays constitute The Ewing Lectures, given by David Daiches at the University of California at Los Angeles in 1967

1971 Publishes *A Third World*. This is a sequel to *Two Worlds* and provides an account of the fourteen years that David Daiches spent in the USA. In this memoir, Daiches describes his American years and his connections with the 'New Critics', whose critical approach to the understanding of literature and to literary analysis was to influence significantly the way literature and literary studies were subsequently taught in the UK

1973 Publishes *Charles Edward Stuart: the life and times of Bonnie Prince Charlie*

1975 Publishes *Was*, a semi-autobiographical celebration of memory, imagination, literature and language

1976 Honorary LittD Brown University, USA
Docteur, *honoris causa*, Sorbonne
Hon DLitt, University of Edinburgh

1977 Death of his wife Isobel

Honorary Fellow, Sunderland Polytechnic

1978 Hon DLitt, University of Sussex

1980 DUniv, University of Stirling

Chairman of the panel of judges of The Booker Prize. Prize awarded to William Golding for his *Rites of Passage*

1980–86 Director, The Institute for Advanced Studies in the Humanities, University of Edinburgh

1981 Appointed to an honorary Professorship in the Department of English Studies, University of Stirling

Elected Fellow of The Royal Society of Edinburgh

1982–86 Appointed President of The Saltire Society

1983 Invited by the University of Edinburgh to give the Gifford Lectures. Past holders of this lectureship include Hannah Arendt, A. J. Ayer, Henri Bergson, A. C. Bradley, John Dewey, Dean Inge, William James, Sir James Frazer, Iris Murdoch, Alfred North Whitehead, Steven Runciman, Albert Schweitzer, Paul Tillich and Arnold Toynbee. Daiches's lectures–*God and the Poets*–is published the following year. Reviewing this book in The *TLS*,

C. H. Sisson comments on the 'remarkable and unusual qualifications' of Daiches as the Gifford Lecturer, and his being the 'first to concentrate on the thoughts of poets about the nature and existence of God'

1984 Appointed Vice-Chairman of the Advisory Board of The Edinburgh Edition of the Waverley Novels, of which Daiches has been described as 'the academic godfather'

1986 Publishes, with Peter Jones and Jean Jones, *A Hotbed of Genius: the Scottish Enlightenment, 1730–1790*

1987 Hon DLitt, University of Glasgow

1988 Awarded the first Lifetime Achievement Award of The Eighteenth-century Scottish Studies Society

1989 Awarded The Fletcher of Saltoun Award for services to Scotland

Dottore *in honorem*, University of Bologna

1990 DUniv, Guelph University, USA

1991 Appointed Commander of the Most Excellent Order of the British Empire

Contributes brilliant introductory essay, '*Boswell's Ambiguities*' to Greg Clingham's *New Light on Boswell*, Cambridge University Press

1994 *Ebb-Tide*, a trio and quartet by Robert Louis Stevenson and Lloyd Osbourne, with an introduction by David Daiches

Publishes *A Weekly Scotsman and Other Poems*, with a foreword by George Bruce and a portrait by Emilio Coia

1995 Appointed Chairman of the Advisory Board of The Stirling / South Carolina Research Edition of The Collected Works of James Hogg

1997 Second edition of *Two Worlds*, with a foreword by David Daiches and an additional essay, '*Promised Lands*'

Contributes an essay, '*Robert Burns: The Tightrope Walker*' to Kenneth Simpson's *Love and Liberty – a bicentenary celebration*

2002 *Bonnie Prince Charlie* re-issued as a Classic Penguin

JOYCE GUNN-CAIRNS

Joyce Gunn-Cairns is a graduate of both the University of Aberdeen, where she studied German and Comparative Religion, and of the Edinburgh College of Art.

A representational painter, her work is mostly figure-based. She specialises in 'literary portraiture' and is interested in making drawings of a sitter over an extended period, from which a body of work emerges, conveying the depths of the sitter and the relationship that develops or evolves between sitter and artist. Joyce drew the poet Tom Scott (1918–1995) in the last ten years of his life. Concurrently, she made many drawings of the churchman Lord (George) MacLeod of Fuinary (1985–1991). Joyce has also made drawings of the Scottish poet Tessa Ransford and is working on a series of drawings of Richard Holloway, former Bishop of Edinburgh, and the Scottish painter Earl Haig. She has also just begun making a series of drawings of the writer A. L. Kennedy.

Over the past ten years, the Scottish National Portrait Gallery has acquired from Joyce many of her portraits and drawings for its permanent collection of 'Eminent Scots'.

Joyce exhibits regularly at the annual exhibitions of The Royal Scottish Academy, The Royal Scottish Society of Painters in Watercolour and The Royal Glasgow Institution. She is a professional member of The Society of Scottish Artists and sits on its Council. She is also a Director of The Exhibiting Societies of Scottish Artists, a registered Scottish Charity whose function is to promote contemporary Scottish art at home and abroad through education and to ensure the long-term safe return of members societies to The Playfair Galleries on the Mound, where they have held their annual exhibitions for over a century.

MICHAEL LISTER

Michael Lister is a graduate of the University of Stirling. An occasional contributor to various literary publications, Michael is also a promoter and supporter of the arts in Scotland.

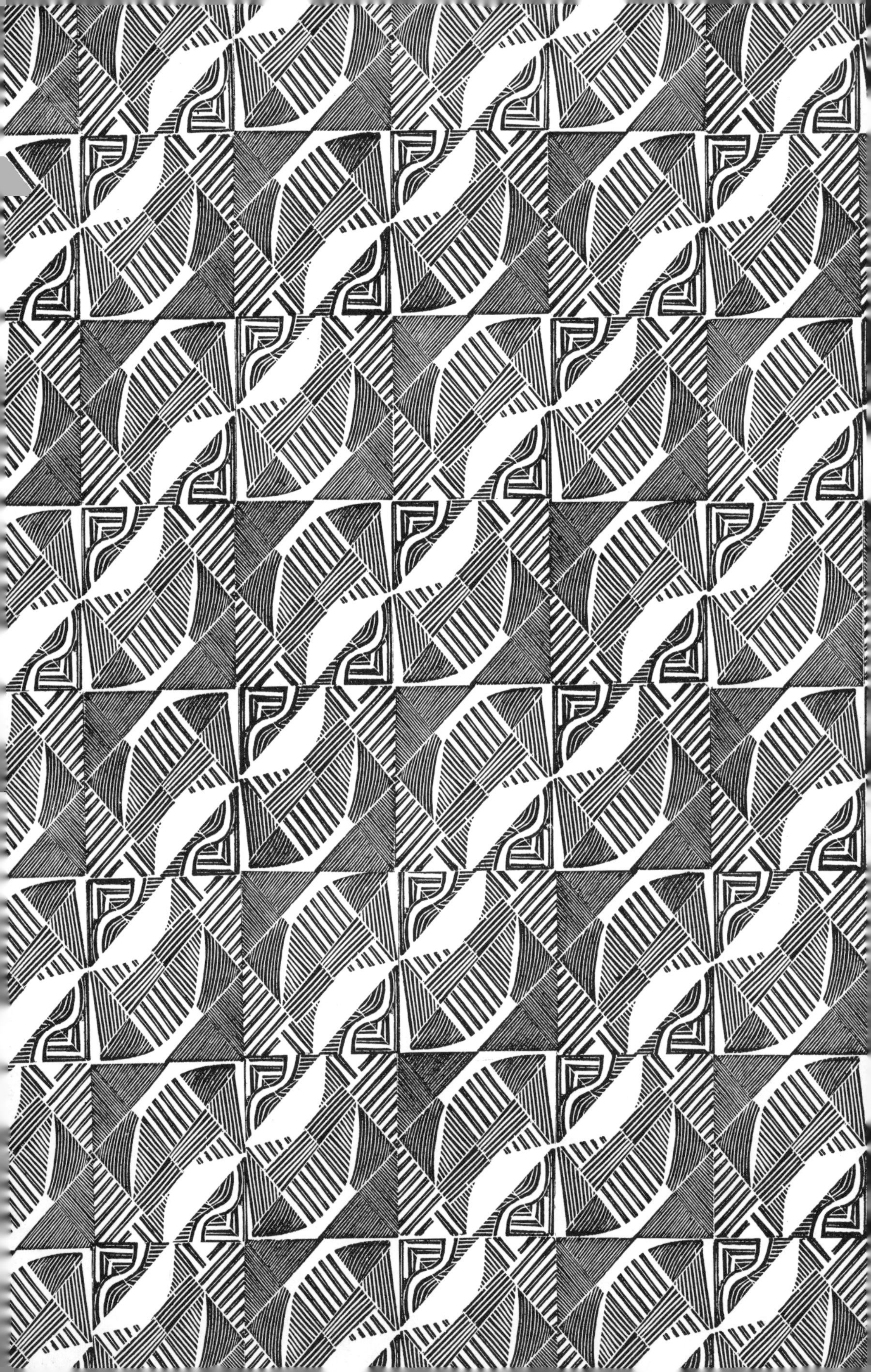